Coupling

Coupling

Poems by

Carolynn Kingyens

Cover design by Shay Culligan

ISBN: 978-1-63980-054-4

Kelsay Books
502 South 1040 East, A-119
American Fork, Utah 84003
Kelsaybooks.com

For Rob, Esmé, and Eloise:
I love you always.

Acknowledgments

Red Eft Review: "Nantucket," "Revival," "In Sickness,"
"Compartmentalize," "Alone Now," "Providence,"
"Driftwood," "Coupling," "Sunday Brunch," "Shadow &
Light"

Doug Holder's Blogspot: "Revival" included in *Poems During
the Plague Series*

The Somerville Times: "Compartmentalize"

The Orange Room Review: "The Safety of Sidewalks"

Street Light Press: "Ghost Peppers"

Glass: A Journal of Poetry: "Vacation Bible School"

Across the Margin: "Miracles are Possible"

Across the Margin: "For Oona," a poem from Kingyens' short
story, "For Oona"

The Potomac: "Discovery"

Contents

China all the way to New York
I can feel the distance getting close
You're right next to me, but I need an airplane
I can feel the distance as you breathe

"China," by Tori Amos
Little Earthquakes

Nantucket

I cannot find
the synonym
for strange;
or stranger still,
the synonym
for misery,
the dampest
place on earth:
Nantucket
in November,
when the cold,
coastal rain
causes the dullest
of aches
deep in the bones
no fire—
real or imagined
can quell.

Revival

I remember the big top,
the big, white tent
we could eye
from as far
as Knights Road;
me in the middle seat
of my father's black
70's Buick,
on the lap of one
of my older siblings—
a hard stop
away from going
through the windshield.

The big top had been
a mirage though:
No circus.
No bag of peanuts.
No fire-eaters.
No pungent smell
of elephant dung.

Instead, this big top
was erected
for the Northeast
tent-revival,
some of that old-time
religion
to induce the fear of God,
shake up the complacent life.

I still recall
those scary sermons
on the plagues—
the loud locusts;
the bloody Nile;
the death of Egypt's
beloved, first-born sons,
including Pharaoh's own.

On the last night,
the preacher's sermon
turned to the plagues
to come, "end times"—
Earthquakes.
Famine.
Wars and rumors of wars.
Pestilence.

As in the days of Noah.

Forty years after the big top
revival,
and 102 years
after the Spanish flu,
COVID-19 plagues
the planet
like an ominous shadow
in the shadows.

People are dying alone.

People are slowly drowning
from the cytokine storm,
an immune response
from a build-up of fluid
in their lungs.

People are dying
horrible deaths.

I see no big top
in the distance,
only white, refrigerated
trucks and the vultures
circling above—
this time, it's no mirage.

In Sickness

To know her is to know
the intimate madness
of a junk drawer;
the madness at the bottom
of a carpetbag—
nail clippers,
old ketchup packets,
loose change,
hard candy hard enough
to chip a front tooth—
Not things as much
as thoughts
is how she described the
rambling sensation.

I know a good man
still in love with his
dementia-suffering wife,
even after she'd hurl insults
from a mouth on fire,
thinking he was
her dead father,
who once dropped
her farm kittens,
one by one,
inside a pillowcase,
tied a tight knot
before casually tossing
the crying, moving bag
into the backyard pond.

Why my kittens, Daddy?!
his wife would scream
while pounding
on her husband's chest
under the glow
of the porch light.

He told me this story
over a beer once—
an old man to a young man,
and in that moment
I knew what I had to do.

The Safety of Sidewalks

I remember that feeling
the first time I took
my hands off my pink,
rubber bicycle handles,
that 1984 Huffy
with its plastic
spaghetti-ribbons
flapping in gravity's wind
as I flew d
                    o
                         w
                              n
Academy Road
past parked blue-collar
cars and rusted-out trucks;
past open garage doors
where old men
in plaid shorts
sat on beach chairs
drinking something cold
and brown,
shouting at me
to "Slow Down!"
while they waved
their scabby,
diabetic-bruised arms
in the air, trying in vain
to wave me back
to the safety of sidewalks.

Then, in time,
I learned cause
and effect—

about physics
and consequences,
about what goes up
comes down,
how karma leaves its mark
on all of us
like the way of the wipeout.

I learned lessons on retreat
and first-hand forfeit.

Even now, I am tempted
to defy
while driving
through familiar roads
leading to my quiet
farmhouse
in Shenandoah.

In summer's darkness,
I roll down my windows
and hear the sounds
of hardback insects—
crickets, locusts,
iridescent beetles,
and just before
the wayward bend,
I turn my headlights off
and I'm free again
as I coast these backcountry
roads by memory;
aware of the animal
crossing ahead,
the dairy cattle,

those pearl-black eyes
of deer staring out
in the distance.

Compartmentalize

You got to hear this. World's a hungry place.
And the darkest things are the hungriest,
and they'll eat what shines.
        —Stephen King, *Doctor Sleep*

I wish I could
compartmentalize
like the *REDRUM* boy
in Kubrick's film,
The Shining,
who can lock away
his monsters
in all kinds
of impenetrable,
mental boxes
like the old hag
in Room 237.

Once I imagined you
locked away
in a soundproof room
still squawking
like some mute,
animated chicken:
head bobbing,
wing-arms flailing.

I laughed,
but it was
a nervous laugh.

When the therapist
mentioned enmeshment,
I'd envisioned
a spider web—
intricate as a lace doily
covering an entrance
of a doorway,
waiting for a hapless,
blissful bug
to buzz through
to its inevitable
entrapment:
its iridescent wings
frantically flailing
until the end.

For Oona

The wind howls
from all
my hollow places.

Somewhere a tree
falls in a forest
among a bed
of bugs, moss,
nurse logs.

Personification of Wind

Today, while waiting
for the B-65,
I watched the wind blow
a dead leaf
into animated cartwheels
past my feet;
each point on the leaf—
a brief appendage.

I thought of you
somewhere being wind,
somewhere carrying
your dog-eared copy
of *How to Win Friends*
and Influence People.

A lifetime ago,
I would have moved
with you to hot Texas;
become a sister wife
to your wife,
the three of us,
a temporary, harmonious
family.

Each chore
around your house—
a station of the cross;
that's how far gone I was,
that's how good you were
in bed.

But the truth is
there's a euphemism
in every story.

Hangnail Blues

The most painful
of cuts
are surprisingly small
and innocuous—
take the hangnail;
annoying, at first,
before the morphing,
before the thumb pulsates
into a tiny, murderous
rage-filled heart—
red, angry, full of pus.

You swear pain has
its own heartbeat.

You swear your thumb
will go KABOOM
when casually bumping it,
trying to clasp
your morning mug
of coffee.

Alone Now

Imagine,
for a moment,
a gang
of brown bulls
raging down
the narrowest street
in Spain—
going 'round
with devilish horns
gouging groins;
witnesses wince
at the sight.

Imagine,
for a moment,
being trapped
on a long flight
to Tibet;
a kind stranger
in the seat beside you—
who never shuts up.

By the fifth hour,
your neck begins
to hurt from all
that nodding.

Your normally
warm, genuine
smile begins to
take on the slight,
crazed smirk
of a serial killer.

Imagine,
for a moment,
an insomniac
who tells time
by the stations
of the moon;
by shadows
and streetlights.

Imagine,
for a moment,
your head
in your hands.

Imagine,
for a moment,
your shoulders
shaking in grief.

Imagine,
for a moment,
an invisible Jesus
sitting in the empty chair
beside you.

What am I going to do?
You ask Him.

The house—
quiet as a tomb.

Pleasantries

When I ask you
how you're doing,
tell me to F-OFF!

Tell me you can't see
past tomorrow.

Tell me you sleep
in the nude.

Tell me you're afraid
of what hides
in the shadows.

Tell me you eat
until you feel
all numb inside.

Tell me about
the numbness.

Tell me anything
but *I'm fine;*
anything but *Fine.*

Discovery

No one warns you
about the movement
in marriage,
that slow-motion drift
toward indifference
when even a revenge lay
doesn't rouse
the spouse anymore—
no more slamming
of doors,
no more crying
in parked cars
in front of houses
of his lovers,
waiting for glimpses
of girls
who are always younger
versions of yourself—
leggy, bright-eyed,
too trusting;
the whole, wide world
waiting
at the sacrificial altar
to be opened
and discovered.

Elephants

To get along
in certain circles
sometimes meant
living with elephants.

The smart ones
carried peanuts
inside their pockets.

*I was not one
of the smart ones.*

The day I picked up
a brochure
on teaching English
as a second language
from a school
somewhere in Seoul,
was the day I planned
to run from the elephants
for good.

I'd imagined myself
teaching a class
in a room
above a bibimbap café,
where afterward I'd go
and drink bubble tea
with new friends.

Then I read about dog
markets and bosintang –
a popular dog meat soup,
and changed my mind.

Jimmy Russo told me
six months
before he jumped off
the George Washington Bridge
that my problem was
I didn't know myself;
that...and I talked too much.

"Why are you so afraid
of silence?" Jimmy asked,
before passing me
his cigarette
as we watched the sun
go down
from the Brooklyn Bridge.

Thirty years later,
and I still *talk too much,*
according to my daughter;
still don't know why
I'm so afraid of silence.

At night, when every sound
is another sound
in the dark,
I think about those elephants;
their big and small gifts.

You grow soft in the body
but hard in the face.

You and I know it should be
the other way—
hard in the body,
soft in the face.

Providence

You will marry a woman
so afraid of silence
she'll make small talk
with anyone who'll solicit —
telemarketers,
Jehovah Witnesses,
beggars,
with whomever;
it doesn't matter.

You, on the other hand,
hate small talk,
and aren't afraid
of silence.

But back then,
your differences
were an aphrodisiac.

You — aplomb
and cocksure.

She — the silly sexpot.

Those humid nights
in Providence,
where you'd go
stumbling around
in the dark,
running your clammy hands
over her thoroughbred-thighs.

Back when her pleasure
was your pleasure,
promising a forever passion
like this.

Your voice,
full of future,
swirled with the ambient
buzz of the ceiling fan
as she lay naked
beside you,
under a pool
of sweaty sheets,
casually smoking
a cigarette

Her O-shaped mouth
made a series
of smoke rings
in the dark.

No one tells you
a forever passion
is the grandest
of lies.

Or how there's
a silence
more deafening
than a scream.

Ghost Peppers

Let's string up some lights,
the red chili peppers!
she says, so I go
and retrieve the Cinco
de Mayo box
from the stacked boxes
of decorations
in the corner alcove
of our Harlem apartment.

But it's January, not May,
not even March,
when the color of my face
goes somewhat back
to normal, a little less pink.

The sky—a perpetual
ghost, and here we are
on a Saturday night
stringing up lights
around the fireplace,
around windows,
inside glass vases:
these fat-looking fingers
of diablo—everywhere.

Let's make guacamole!
she says next,
so I head out to Mr. Melon,
a 24-hour health food store

at the corner,
to buy a few soft avocados,
and a lime.

Outside, my Nordic nose
goes numb in a matter
of seconds;
my face for sure—
pink.

I look up
at the far-right corner
of our pre-war building
to see the windows
of our apartment
already aglow in red;
inside—a January inferno.

Driftwood

No one tells you
how it will end,
or when you know
you've reached
a rock-bottom heart,
where I imagine
echo and void dwell
in these badlands,
in these drylands,
a tumbleweed of memory—
your dress socks
rolled into a ball
in some dust bunny-corner;
loose change
atop your dresser;
a slamming door
a room away;
a long shower;
another lukewarm meal
in relative silence.
Yet we still cling
to that other
in this darkness;
our driftwood-bodies
busy becoming one
in this bed,
in this flood
of our making.

Coupling

I listened to you retell it
to our new friends
from our new church,
the story of how
we first met.

I sat in silence
with my hands
under the table,
wrapping my dirty,
cloth napkin
around a small fist.

Your version of events
were tidy and clean,
when you said
you knew I was the woman
you were destined to marry
the moment you saw me
in your doorway,
punctual as always,
asking for Harrison,
my blind date,
and your perpetually late
roommate.

Our new friend, Allison,
cocked her head,
cooing out
a falsetto's squeal
to her mute husband:
Isn't that romantic?

If she only knew our truth;
you had no interest
in wanting to marry me
the day I showed up
in your messy doorway
with empty chip bags
and T-shirts
strewn across wood floors,
it had nothing to do
with coupling.

I was ripe, hot,
willing to please—
not yet the bitch
you would later marry.

I was naïve in a white,
strapless sundress,
and long hair
still shower-damp,
smelling of mint
and clover.

I let you kiss my mouth,
my neck, my back
in your bedroom;

let you hide me
inside your closet
when Harrison rapped
on your door,
asking about a girl.

Happiness is
feeding the pigeons.

No lie.

Sunday Brunch

Justin called himself
a feminist,
and promised me
he'd do the laundry
and I'd drink the beer;
said he made
a mean lasagna—
a recipe he'd learned
from his dying mother.

She had a partner
named Sonya,
and they were still
blissfully in love
after twenty-five years
of raising
a fatherless boy
into a young man;
instilling in him compassion
for both sexes,
not just his own.

I was curious
when the invitation came
written on a napkin
from feminist-Justin,
asking me to join
the three of them
for Sunday brunch
in a sunroom
built off the kitchen,
an addition
a year before
his mother's diagnosis.

They welcomed me
into their intimate tribe
of books, lilacs,
earthy accents,
of *A Prairie Home
Companion*
trailing off
in the background
among warm conversation
and acceptance.

I'd watch
their gentle exchanges,
glances
between a mother
and her woman,
glances
between these women
to Justin and to me.

And the whole,
sun-filled room
was palpable
in these moments
of laughter
and cancer,
of Far East travels
and trinkets—
in stories about
coming home
and being home.

Shadow & Light

Shadow:

He once called her
his better half—
before the arrival
of children,
the car payments,
and bankruptcy;
before the sex addiction,
the mistress,
and murder
in the middle of the night—
"a familicide,"
they called it
on the six o'clock news.

It always starts with a seed,
a snag, some technicality—
a lust so small
you have to squint
to see it.

Light:

Now the heroes,
those firefighters,
who'd storm
the Twin Towers,
carrying the weight

48

of breath in tanks,
before climbing
an infinity of stairs
to an awaiting doom.

Or how that rookie cop,
the son of a veteran,
delivered a baby boy
in the backseat
of a beat-up Buick,
outside Vegas,
gently placing the
wet, screaming newborn
inside the warmth
of his coat,
before bringing him
close to the heart.

The wisdom of a longshoreman:
Water always wins.

Vacation Bible School

We sang songs
in Vacation Bible School
about how Jesus
loved the little children
of the world:
Red and yellow,
black and white
they are precious
in His sight,
the song goes.

And we sang songs
about Father Abraham,
and his many sons,
marching around the room
in perfect unison:
all of us, soldiers for Christ.

We drank Jim Jones-colored
punch and ate *no-frills*
butter cookies;
finger painted Noah
and his rescued animals:
elephants, giraffes,
their heads, two at a time,
sticking out round holes—
windows we created
on paper
in the brown-colored ark.

We painted a bluish-green
flood with bloated bodies
sprinkled into swirls
of aquamarine.

For added drama,
Paul Simmons drew a hand
reaching out
from under water
like Peter did to Jesus
when he started sinking
due to lack of faith.

Years later, Timmy Ainsley
would shoot himself
in the mouth
after he came out
to his parents
about his love
for Paul Simmons.

There was a rumor
some blood
and brain tissue
landed on Timmy's
Top Gun poster,
the one where Tom Cruise
mugs beside a motorcycle.

And I heard little Regina
Hopely, Bethel's Christmas
Pageant Mary,
became a meth addict;
covered in sores
and begging, like Lazarus,
on the cold streets
of Fishtown.

Somewhere a hustler
is recanting his woes
to a sucker.

Slumming

While your bourgeois
girlfriends were in Paris
studying art history
and the French language,
you were studying
French kissing
from an illiterate boy
with no thumb,
who'd lost it
in a sawmill accident;
how you kissed
his waxy, pink scar,
stuck the nub
in your mouth;
it was the most real
you'd ever felt.

So imagine
what he thought
when you walked by him
in the parking lot,
your perfect ponytail
swaying—
waving goodbye.

Your strong, tan arms
full of books,
layered in front
of your chest
like collegiate armor—

knowing he couldn't read,
make out those
long vowels:
he wasn't going
where you were going.

Miracles are Possible

Hot as a hair dryer
in your face
Hot as a handbag
and a can of mace
New York
I just got a place
in New York

"New York"—U2

What I love most
about this resourceful,
industrial hustle-city
is the unspoken agreement
that anything can happen
at any time.

Miracles are possible here.

Maybe that stranger
who you will sit next to
on the same Central Park bench
is just an angel
in disguise,
or a reincarnated,
laid-back Lennon,
who may acknowledge
your presence
with a badass tip
of his hat
like in a foreign
espionage movie,

where information
is passed
through covered coughs
and left-behind briefcases.

On the days
when I'm mindful enough,
I can hear the faint call
to prayer
over the incessant honking,
over the subway cars
rumbling down
in Dostoyevsky's
underground.

Somewhere a lover
is feeding a lover.

Tikri

He takes me here
to show me
what wind can do
on the farmland
of the goddesses,
who hand-pick crops
with hands of henna:
collecting their harvest
in flaxseed satchels
and wicker-braided baskets
overflowing with lentils,
millet, coarse grains.

Watch, he said,
pointing East
as the wind
kicks up funnels
of colorful sari scarves
in yellow,
orange,
pink,
indigo—
now suspended above
their bent, bejeweled brows,
aglow in the slant
of sun—
these flickering silk flames
in the fields
of the blessed.

Somewhere a dog
lies dead in a ditch
off a long stretch
of dark highway
that straddles
two states
to nowhere.

Leaving

First you hear the sound
of a zipper zipping,
the meows of a cat,
and then the sound
of dry kibble
cascading into a small
metal bowl;
then you listen for
the jingling of keys
and somewhere a door
is closing.

About the Author

Carolynn Kingyens was born and raised in Northeast Philadelphia.

Her debut book of poetry *Before the Big Bang Makes a Sound* (Kelsay Books) was released in January 2020. In February 2020, Barnes & Noble (Brooklyn) did an Instagram post, writing: *Contemporary, urban, and impassioned, Carolynn Kingyens' poetry resonates with a darkening echo still felt long after the first read.*

In addition to poetry, Kingyens writes essays, book and film reviews, flash fiction and short stories. She recently completed her first manuscript collection of short stories entitled *Soundtrack Stories.*

Today, she lives in New York and Canada with her husband and their two beautiful and creative daughters.

www.ingramcontent.com/pod-product-compliance
Lightning Source LLC
Chambersburg PA
CBHW031153090426
42738CB00008B/1308